# Minecraft Dungeons:
## Beginner's Guide

SHOOT THE SKELETON GU
A CRY FOR HE

21st Century Skills **INNOVATION LIBRARY**

Josh Gregory

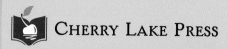

Published in the United States of America by Cherry Lake Publishing Group
Ann Arbor, Michigan
www.cherrylakepublishing.com

Reading Adviser: Beth Walker Gambro, MS, Ed., Reading Consultant, Yorkville, IL

**Cherry Lake Press** is an imprint of Cherry Lake Publishing Group.

Library of Congress Cataloging-in-Publication Data has been filed and is available at catalog.loc.gov

Cherry Lake Publishing Group would like to acknowledge the work of the Partnership for 21st Century Learning, a Network of Battelle for Kids. Please visit http://www.battelleforkids.org/networks/p21 for more information.

Printed in the United States of America
Corporate Graphics

**Josh Gregory** is the author of more than 200 books for kids. He has written about everything from animals to technology to history. A graduate of the University of Missouri–Columbia, he currently lives in Chicago, Illinois.

# Contents

# CHAPTER 1

# A Different Kind of Minecraft

*Minecraft* is famous for letting players shape the world in any way they want. Anything in the game can be destroyed or built up in limitless combinations. Dedicated players have built everything from vast, detailed cities to functioning computers, musical instruments, and transportation systems.

This nearly endless potential for creativity has been a big part of *Minecraft*'s success. Players have been enjoying the game for well over a decade, and today it is the best-selling video game of all time. But fans know that there is much more to *Minecraft* than just building. It is also a game about action, adventure, and exploration. In between constructing incredible buildings, players can explore massive underground dungeons and battle fearsome monsters. They can **craft** new weapons and other gear, and they can wander the world in search of interesting sights. For many players, this part of the game is even more exciting than building.

In 2018, Mojang, the team of **developers** behind *Minecraft*, announced that they were working on a brand-new *Minecraft* game. It wouldn't be a sequel to the original. Instead, it would be a new take on the *Minecraft* world, focusing on action and adventure instead of building. The name of the game would be *Minecraft Dungeons*.

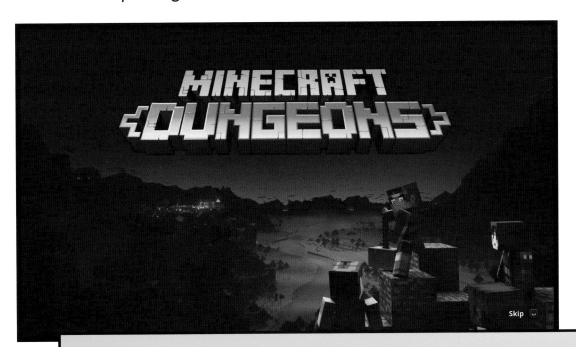

The graphical style of *Minecraft Dungeons* will be very familiar to players of the original *Minecraft*.

# What You Need to Play

Interested in trying *Minecraft Dungeons* for yourself? Getting started is easy as long as you have a modern gaming console or a Windows PC. If you do, the only other thing you need is a copy of the game, either on disc or as a digital download.

Some people prefer different ways of controlling the game. If you are using a gaming console, you will probably play *Minecraft Dungeons* using a standard controller. PC players can use a controller too, if they like. However, many of them prefer a mouse and keyboard for this style of game. Using a mouse will make it easier to target specific enemies during hectic combat situations. But if you're not used to playing games that way, it might take some getting used to.

From early gameplay videos, fans could see that *Minecraft Dungeons* would be part of the dungeon crawler **genre**. Dungeon crawlers have been popular since the 1970s and 1980s, with some of the earliest PC games helping to establish the formula for the style. In a typical dungeon crawler, a player starts out with a weak character with very basic gear. They must venture out into a dangerous world and defeat enemies to grow stronger and get better equipment. This allows them to take on tougher and tougher challenges.

There is a lot of variety in the dungeon crawler genre. Some dungeon crawlers are role-playing games where players battle enemies using turn-based strategic combat. Others are fast-paced action games. Some take place in a **first-person** view, while others show the action from overhead. Some are single-player games, while others encourage players to partner with friends online. Many dungeon crawlers allow players to explore randomly generated worlds. This means the game's

*Minecraft Dungeons* will send you into one dangerous environment after another, each packed with tough enemies to battle.

Some parts of *Minecraft Dungeons* levels, such as locked doors, will have the same layout every time you play.

levels are arranged differently every time a player starts a new game. But on the other hand, some feature carefully crafted levels that stay the same every time.

*Minecraft Dungeons* is most similar to games such as the popular *Diablo* series. It is played from a top-down view and its combat requires fast reflexes. Parts of its levels are randomly generated, while others were carefully designed by the game's developers. The game is set in the universe of the original *Minecraft*, and the setting should be very familiar to anyone who has enjoyed the series before, with enemies like creepers and skeletons wandering around blocky, brightly colored environments.

Unlike the original *Minecraft*, *Minecraft Dungeons* features a storyline that unfolds as players make their way through the game's levels. It tells the tale of Archie, a villager who discovers a magical device

Each mission in *Minecraft Dungeons* starts off with a short movie that advances the game's story.

called the Orb of Dominance. This turns him into a powerful villain called the Arch-Illager. He builds an army of monsters and starts trying to take over the *Minecraft* world. Players take on the role of a hero out to stop the Arch-Illager and restore peace to the land.

When *Minecraft Dungeons* finally released in May 2020, fans were excited to see how it had turned out. Would it be as fun as the original game? How would it compare to other dungeon crawlers? Luckily, they had

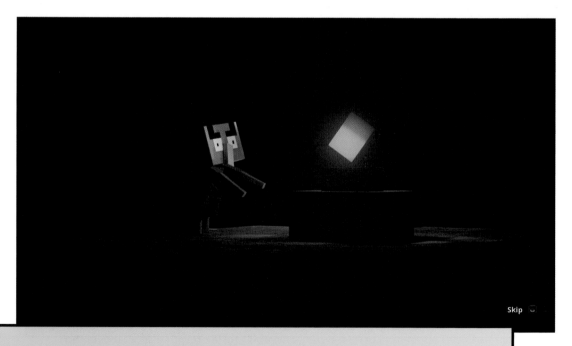

The mysterious Orb of Dominance is a magical device that sets off the events of *Minecraft Dungeons*.

nothing to worry about. Critics agreed that the game was a fun take on the classic dungeon crawler formula. Many of them noted that it was actually a perfect introduction to the genre for players who had never tried it before. Its simple combat and gear systems are easy to learn. However, there is also plenty of depth for players who really want to dig into the game.

Are you ready to set off on your own *Minecraft Dungeons* adventure?

# CHAPTER 2

# Diving into the Dungeon

When you start up *Minecraft Dungeons* for the first time, you'll be treated to a long scene setting up the game's story. After that, it's time to start a new game and dive into the world of dungeon crawling. Your first task will be to create a character. This is a very simple process. All you need to do is choose a **skin** and press "Done." A skin is just the way your character looks. It does not have any other effect on the game. You can also change it every time you start playing, so don't worry too much about which one you pick.

Once the game begins, you'll get another story scene, then it's time to start playing for real. Tips will appear on the screen explaining how to move your character around and perform basic actions. Just like in most dungeon crawlers, you won't start out with much in the way of gear or abilities. All you'll be able to do is run, swing your sword, and dodge enemy attacks.

Move along the path, attacking enemies as you go. Keep an eye on the big red heart at the bottom of the screen. This is your health meter. If it starts to drop too low, press the button to drink a potion. This will restore your health. However, you'll need to wait a while before you use it again. This means you need to time your potion use carefully. Learning this timing is an important skill if you want to make it far into the game.

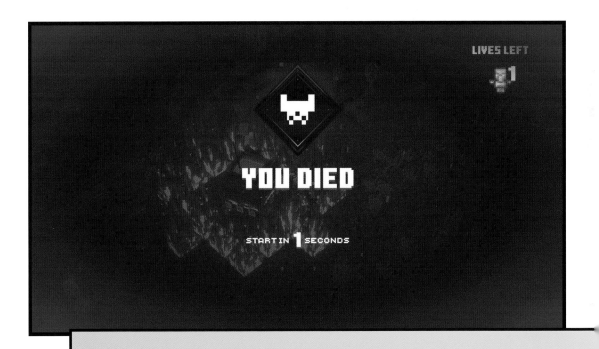

You'll see this screen a lot if you aren't careful about using your healing potion at the right time.

ARROW BUNDLE
A small bundle of arrows

Picking up your first bundle of arrows will give you the chance to start using ranged attacks. You'll need these to take out enemies with their own ranged attacks.

As you move through the game's first level, you'll soon pick up a bundle of arrows. This important tool gives you a ranged attack so you can strike enemies from a distance. Knowing when to use ranged and **melee** attacks is a major part of combat in *Minecraft Dungeons*. Ranged attacks allow you to hit enemies that are out of reach and enemies that use ranged attacks of their own. These attacks are also good for taking out dangerous enemies before they get close enough to hit you. However, each ranged attack uses up your supply of arrows. This means you can't keep using them unless you keep picking up arrows. Melee attacks tend to be stronger, and you can always keep swinging your weapon no matter what else happens.

You'll probably notice a yellow arrow marker on your screen as you move along the main path. This marker

# *Playing Together*

Much like the original *Minecraft*, *Minecraft Dungeons* gives players the option to go on adventures together. Up to four players at once can join a game. They can play together in person, sharing a screen and using the same game console. They can also meet up online. When playing online, players do not need to be using the same type of gaming system. For example, this means someone using an Xbox can play alongside friends who are playing on a PC, Nintendo Switch, or PlayStation.

The more players that are in a level, the tougher the enemies will be. This keeps the game challenging, so players cannot simply gang up on enemies and plow through levels. Loot drops are also adjusted based on how many players are in a game. This ensures that everyone will find useful gear.

will always show you the way to go to move toward the end of a level. This means you will rarely get lost as you explore dungeons. You can also bring up a map at any time if you are confused about where to go.

Sometimes your **objective** in a level will simply be to get from one location to another. Other times, you might need to complete various goals before you can move ahead, such as finding a key, defeating an enemy, or rescuing captured villagers. The game will

Many objectives will require you to find and click on an object somewhere in the level.

always let you know what your next objective is, so your goal should always be clear.

Once you complete the first level of *Minecraft Dungeons*, you will find yourself in an area called the camp. You'll return to this location after completing each level, or any time you are defeated. From the camp, you can choose which level you would like to play next by heading to the stone table marked "Mission Select." As you progress through the game, you will also rescue a number of merchants who will start hanging out around the camp. These characters will sell you a variety of new gear and can help make your adventure much easier.

Are you simply looking to make your way through the main storyline of *Minecraft Dungeons*? Making progress is very simple: All you need to do is keep completing dungeons. New ones will open up as you move ahead. Eventually, you will find yourself face-to-face with the Arch-Illager!

# CHAPTER 3

# Stronger and Stronger

Seasoned dungeon crawler fans know that making it to the end of a game's story is only part of the fun. The real challenge comes in trying to build the most powerful characters and find the rarest, most interesting loot.

There are two basic measurements of how strong your character is in *Minecraft Dungeons*. The first is your character's level. This starts out at one and goes up gradually as you defeat enemies. Each enemy you defeat gives you a certain amount of experience points. The tougher the enemy, the more experience you will get. As you gain experience, the purple bar at the bottom of the screen will fill up. Once this bar is completely full, your character level will go up by one. This will give you an enchantment point, which you can use to strengthen your gear.

Gear is grouped into four major categories in *Minecraft Dungeons*. Armor protects your character against enemy attacks. Melee weapons increase your melee attack abilities. Ranged weapons increase your ranged attacks. And finally, artifacts are items that give your character a special ability. For example, one artifact might turn all of your ranged attacks into fire arrows. Another might give you access to a special healing spell. You can equip up to three different artifacts at a time and use them during combat.

Each time you level up, your health will be instantly filled to the maximum. This comes in handy if you level up during a tough fight!

How do you find new gear? The main way is by defeating enemies, opening treasure chests, and completing dungeons. From time to time, enemies will drop armor, weapons, and other useful things when they are defeated. Simply pick them up and open your **inventory** to swap out your gear. You can look at each item's stats and decide which combination of gear works best. Each weapon works differently. Some can attack at different speeds. Some can hit enemies from

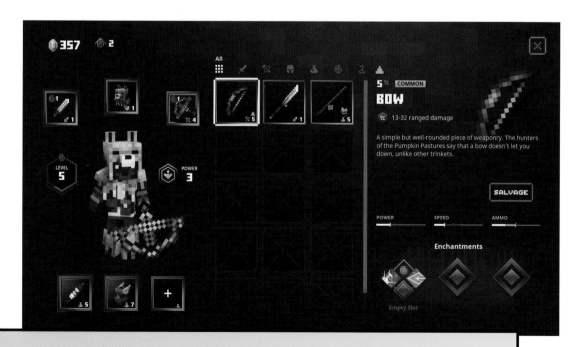

Choosing the right gear will allow you to take on different types of challenges.

farther away. You'll have to experiment to see which ones you like best.

Each melee weapon, ranged weapon, and set of armor can be improved through enchantments. Different pieces of gear have different enchantments available. You will need to spend the enchantment points you get from leveling up to unlock these enchantments. Each one will give your gear special properties. For example, you might enchant a sword that restores health each time you hit an enemy. Or you might create armor that damages any enemies that get too close to you. There are all kinds of enchantments in the game, and finding good ones can completely change the way you play.

It's best not to enchant every piece of gear you find. You'll quickly run out of points if you do things this way. Instead, enchant the items you will use most. Also, choose enchantments wisely. It's no use spending points on ones that aren't much use with your play style. The combination of your character's gear, enchantments is often called a "build." Each character build is slightly different, and expert players work to try to find the most effective builds possible. Some builds might focus on extremely powerful ranged attacks.

Others might result in characters that can take huge amounts of damage without being defeated. It all depends how you want to play the game. Don't be afraid to experiment and see what you like best.

The other measurement of your character's strength is their power level. This rating measures the average strength of each piece of gear your character is currently wearing. The game uses your character's

# Take Your Time

*Minecraft Dungeons* is a big game. It can take a long time to build a character powerful enough to take on the game's biggest challenges. Don't try to rush through, and don't feel bad if you aren't ready to tackle the toughest dungeons right away. Dungeon crawler fans know that sometimes a big part of the fun is "grinding" for experience points or to find just the right gear to handle the next big challenge. Some players might spend hours seeking out a weapon with a certain set of enchantments or experimenting with different combinations of artifacts to see what works best.

power level to guess how difficult each dungeon will be when you are on the level select screen. In general, you should not attempt dungeons where your character doesn't meet the recommended power level. Instead, you should go back to previous levels and improve your gear until your character is strong enough to take on the challenge.

You can check out all kinds of information about a level before you jump in and start exploring.

Replaying levels is highly encouraged in *Minecraft Dungeons*. After finishing a level for the first time, you will have the option to change the difficulty each time you replay it. There are several difficulties for each dungeon. Each one offers tougher and tougher enemies, but the rewards also become greater. You'll have a chance to get more experience points, and better gear will drop when you defeat enemies. There

LEVEL COMPLETE
**SOGGY SWAMP**

LEVEL
5

Poonis85
**95**
Arrows Hit

**MISSION SUMMARY**

| Mobs Defeated | Healing done | Damage Taken | Damage Dealt |
| --- | --- | --- | --- |
| **56%** | **57** | **824** | **6,467** |

Each time you finish a level, you will see a screen showing how well you did.

⬧ **11** ⬧ RARE

**CORRUPTED BEACON**

The Corrupted Beacon holds immense power within. It waits
for the moment to unleash its wrath.

**TO CAMP**

You will also receive a new gear item each time you finish a level.

is no way to get everything in a level on the first try.
You'll need to go back multiple times if you really want
to get everything the game has to offer.

# CHAPTER 4

# The Next Steps

By now, you probably have a pretty good feel for how to play *Minecraft Dungeons*. Maybe you are even starting to think about creative new builds you'd like to try. But how do you start tracking down just the right gear? One helpful thing is to unlock all of the game's merchants.

Once you start rescuing merchants from various dungeons, they will set up shop in the camp. Between missions, you can visit them to purchase new gear or improve your current items. If you're having a hard time finding merchants, check the Mission Select screen. Levels where merchants are trapped will have a small icon that looks like a shop stall. The merchant will be hidden somewhere in the level, so search carefully.

To purchase things from merchants, you'll need plenty of emeralds. These valuable gems can be found all over as you make your way through dungeons. You'll find them by opening up treasure chests or smashing other containers. And in between levels, you can almost always find some emeralds around your camp.

You can also gain emeralds by salvaging gear you don't want. This is a simple process. Open up your inventory, then highlight the items you want to

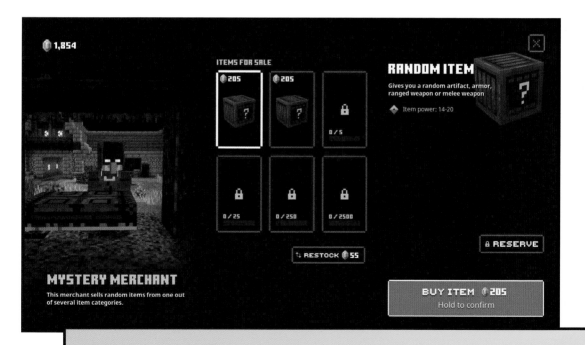

The Mystery Merchant sells boxes you can only open after you buy them. That means you won't see what you get until after you pay.

get rid of. Select the option to salvage it, and the item will be destroyed. In exchange, you'll receive some emeralds. Stronger items will give you more emeralds when you salvage them. And if your items were enchanted, you'll get enchantment points back from salvaging them. This frees you up to experiment with enchantments on better gear.

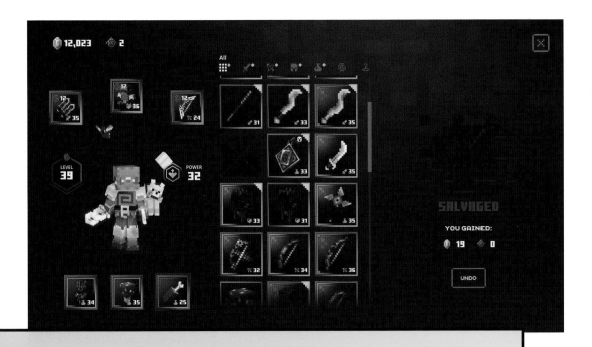

You should generally salvage any items you don't plan on using.

Pull up your on-screen map to see where you haven't been yet in a level.

As you explore, you don't need to follow the yellow marker strictly all the time. This marker will only point you toward the end of a level. But there are always other paths and secrets to discover. Keep a close eye on your map as you move through levels. You'll see that there are paths that don't lead toward the level's goal. Try them out to see what you find. Usually there are at least some emeralds or a treasure chest when you search off the beaten path. Sometimes it's something even better!

If you're looking for more secrets and treasure to uncover, look at the Mission Select screen. Just like hidden merchants, these things will be marked on the map so you know which levels to find them in. Selecting a level will also show you a list of all the gear that could possibly drop when you defeat enemies. So if you're looking for a specific type of weapon, you can find the level where it is available and replay until it drops.

## An Even Bigger Adventure

Are you running out of things to do in the main storyline of *Minecraft Dungeons*? If you want to keep playing, there is plenty of downloadable content (DLC) available to expand the game. Each pack of DLC adds new dungeons to explore, new enemies to battle, and new gear to pick up. So far, Mojang has released six of these DLC packs. Each one costs a few dollars. Be sure to ask a parent before purchasing any DLC for your games!

It's time to dive in and start battling your way through the world of *Minecraft Dungeons*!

With this knowledge, you should have no trouble getting started on your *Minecraft Dungeons* adventure. But there is still plenty more to learn, and the only way to see everything the game has to offer is to get out there and start playing. What are you waiting for?

## GLOSSARY

**craft** (KRAFT) to make or build something

**developers** (dih-VEL-uh-purz) people who make video games or other computer programs

**first-person** (FURST-PUR-sun) taking place through the eyes of a character

**genre** (ZHAHN-ruh) a category of similar games, movies, books, or other forms of media

**inventory** (IN-vuhn-toh-ree) a list of the items your character is carrying in a video game

**melee** (MAY-lay) relating to hand-to-hand combat

**objective** (uhb-JEK-tiv) goal

**skin** (SKIN) a different appearance your character can take on in a video game

## FIND OUT MORE

**Books**

Milton, Stephanie. *Guide to Minecraft Dungeons: A Handbook for Heroes*. New York: Del Rey, 2020.

Zeiger, Jennifer. *The Making of Minecraft*. Ann Arbor, MI: Cherry Lake Publishing, 2017.

**Websites**

**Minecraft Dungeons**
*https://www.minecraft.net/en-us/about-dungeons*
Check out the official *Minecraft Dungeons* website for the latest updates on the game.

**Minecraft Dungeons Wiki**
*https://minecraft.fandom.com/wiki/Minecraft_Dungeons*
This fan-created wiki is packed with useful details about *Minecraft Dungeons* and its DLC.

## INDEX